The Moidart Sniper

John (Ton) MacDonald

Fergie MacDonald
with Allan Henderson

D1437889

First published in 2018 by
Fergie MacDonald
Mingarry, Moidart, Acharacle, Argyll PH36 4JX
Tel: 01967 431662
Email: fergiemacd@hotmail.co.uk
Website: www.fergiemacdonald.com

Printed by For The Right Reasons, Inverness
fortherightreasons@rocketmail.com

ISBN 9 781527 227675

Contents

Foreword – Lord Lovat

It is with much pride that I write this foreword to The Moidart Sniper, which tells the story of the Lovat Scouts Sharp Shooters and their short but illustrious part in the Great War, in the centennial year of its conclusion. The regiment was formed by my great-grandfather, the 14th Lord Lovat, on his return from the Gallipoli Campaign of 1915-16, and consisted of a small detachment of 200 sharpshooters, exceptionally skilled marksmen and telescope experts.

The LSS were trained in Beauly and were an offshoot regiment of the Lovat Scouts, founded by the same great-grandfather during the Second Boer War, and also drew on the natural skills of the stalkers and ghillies of the Scottish Highlands to succeed in warfare. Just these 200 men alone were awarded 50 medals from their short service in the Great War, but little is known of the Lovat Scouts Sharpshooters, as the archive of their heroics was hit by a German bomb in the Second World War, 25 years later. Therefore, we are all particularly indebted to Fergie MacDonald for having taken the time to painstakingly research their lost history, told through the eyes of his own father who served with the regiment.

Simon Fraser, Lord Lovat – Beauly 2018

'I am delighted to be involved in Fergie MacDonald's book about the Lovat Scouts during the First World War, not only because my grandfather was made commanding officer of the Lovat Scouts Sharpshooters in 1917, but also because my father commanded the Lovat Scouts at the end of the Second World War.

Fergie has written an account full of fascinating anecdotes, and the book has been meticulously researched and reflects the views of his father – a soldier at the sharp end. I have no hesitation in commending this book to those interested in military history, and to those who are interested in Lochaber.'

Donald Cameron of Lochiel – Achnacarry, May 2018

'Fergie, we are old friends now, but when we first met, neither of us realised that our family connection went back to 1916. So thanks to you for having the initiative and dedication to correlate your father's Great War experiences in such a devoted and well-researched account.

On a personal level, it gives our MacGillivray family the rare privilege of a first-hand insight into some of the travails endured by my grandfather, Captain John. So thanks to his loyal comrade-in-arms, your father John, for having the foresight and presence of mind to record such events in the turmoil of the front-line, for the benefit of future generations.'

Duncan MacGillivray – Calrossie, May 2018

'I think it's incredible, Fergie, that your father John MacDonald, and my great-grandfather, Captain John MacGillivray, fought together side by side in the trenches during the War, in such an elite unit.

The link that we share here is quite remarkable, and it makes me so proud to be aware of this connection.

Slàinte agus beannachdan leibh uile!'

Iain MacGillivray – Commander of Clan MacGillivray

Fergie MacDonald would like to thank the following people, whose help was invaluable in the compiling of this book:

Duncan and Iain MacGillivray, Calrossie; Donald Cameron of Lochiel; Simon Fraser, Lord Lovat; Donald Fraser, Beauly; Captain Donald Monro, Kinlochmoidart; Nino Stewart, Kinlochmoidart House; Angus Peter MacLean, Kinlochmoidart; Allan Henderson, Mallaig; Iain Ferguson – Lochaber Life, Fort William; Kay MacIver, Acharacle; Rob Fairley, Lochailort; Donna Maguire, Edinburgh; Father Michael MacDonald, South Uist; John Watts, West Lothian; Printsmith, Fort William; Scott MacLennan – Press and Journal, Inverness; John Dye, Dalnabreac, Moidart; Donald Maclean, Dalnabreac and Forres; Iain Thornber, Morvern.

Fergie would also like to thank his family: Maureen, John, Angela, Morven and Emma for all their help and support.

John 'Ton' The Moidart Sniper

Fergie MacDonald

FOREWORD – FERGIE MACDONALD

From the age of 5, I had a very close relationship with my father, who lived to the grand old age of 95. As a child my toy was the sniper's Lee-Enfield .303 calibre rifle that my father somehow managed to take home to Moidart after the war in 1919. On going to school, I spoke no English, just Gaelic. However, to the teacher's astonishment, I did have a limited number of English words which were: rifle, bolt, magazine, trigger, back sight, foresight and aim. Little did I know at that age that my play toy had been an instrument of death in the killing fields of Bapaume, Cambrai, St Quentin and Pérrone in the Somme sector of the Western Front, and Suvla Bay in Gallipoli.

I listened to and noted detailed accounts of events from my father. From enlisting in The Lovat Scouts in 1910 right up to the Armistice in 1918. He talked almost daily about the Great War. I honestly believe he somehow enjoyed being in the thick of it. In Gallipoli, he was dicing with death on a daily basis in the firing line and forward trenches. On the Somme he was very proud to be serving in the newly formed special elite sniper unit, the Lovat Scouts Sharpshooters.

Over the years I collected and tabulated data in the form of letters, personal diary notes, detailed accounts by men who served with him, and reels of tapes detailing events orally recorded by himself.

I have read many books in relation to sniping and observations written by high-ranking officers - all very interesting and informative, but from an officer's perspective. In this book I endeavour to capture and follow the day-to-day life of a West Highland Lovat Scout sniper, engaged at the sharp end in World War One. Facing the enemy in many varied and different circumstances.

I find my father's life then exciting, fascinating, interesting and dangerous. In today's modern world terminology, I would say that from 1914 to 1918, John MacDonald, my father, lived his life in the ultimate fast lane.

JOHN 'TON' MACDONALD – HIS EARLY YEARS

The John MacDonald story begins at Croft Number 27, Mingarry, Moidart. Born in Nitshill, Barrhead, Glasgow in 1893 to parents Esther (Wright) and John MacDonald. Esther was a school teacher of Irish descent and John was a gardener, born in Moss, Moidart, who moved to Barrhead around 1890.

My grandmother's family had come over from Tipperary and settled in Paisley. Her father was a miner, but Esther was lucky enough to go to college and become a school teacher, finding herself down in Campbeltown for her first job.

My father was their first child born – they went on to have a family of seven – and he took seriously ill because of malnutrition when he was three years old.

It seems that my grandfather got mixed up with the wrong guys. He took to alcohol and he took to gambling; mostly through greyhound racing. He had been a top class gardener around the big houses of Glasgow, but rather than come home with his wage packet on a Friday, he would go socialising, and the family would not see him until Sunday, by which point he would have no money left, meaning that the family often went without food.

My father in particular was not getting the nutrition he should have, hence the reason he became dangerously ill.

When he recovered, his Aunt Charlotte called to see the family in Nitshill on her way to holiday at home in Moidart. She collected young John, having decided that a holiday in the Highlands would be of great benefit to his recovery. Charlotte was in service with the Marquess of Bute in Rothesay, and of course had to return after her holiday. Her sister Ann

1

decided that young John should remain for a further period, and that his father would collect him at a later date.

There were three attempts to get him back to Glasgow. Each time he would be dressed for the journey south, but in a flash he would break loose and hide in a cave in the Mingarry wood, remaining there all day, making sure his father was away on the boat. He would then appear back at croft 27 to the delight of his Auntie Ann. Further attempts were made, but Auntie Ann eventually insisted that John would stay with her and never go back to Glasgow.

I believe my grandfather came north once more, a number of years later, to visit his sister. I think things went fine at first between himself and my father, but then, one day, he said to his sister Ann: 'Well, I'll be off, but I'm happy that I'll be able to take over here, and you'll be leaving the croft to me,' but Ann said no, that the croft would be left to the one that it should be left to, and that was John.

It seems that my grandfather took this news very badly and was all for digging his heels in, but my father went upstairs, got my grandfather's bag, his clothes and his boots and threw the whole lot out of the window, telling him that he never wanted to see him again, and he never did. What a sad end to a father and son's relationship.

As Auntie Ann was a spinster, my father would help her on the croft and became good at it. Cows, calves, hay, corn, potatoes, digging drains, fencing and many other chores became part of daily life, coupled with school, church, cutting peat, sawing trees for firewood and keeping the household and the byre topped up with water from the well.

Just like me, my father had quite a stammer. It wasn't as bad as mine, and he must have grown out of it, as he could go on talking all day. That was one of the faults that everyone found with him; they couldn't get him to stop talking, so he must have found a way of dealing with his stammer.

In his early years he couldn't get his tongue round the letter 'J,' so rather than say 'John', he would say 'Ton.' That name stuck to him all his life – Ton. In Gallipoli he was called Ton, as the Lovat Scouts who served with him were all from his own home area of Moidart. However, on joining the Lovat Scouts Sharpshooters nobody knew the name *Ton*, hence he was known as John, but most people knew him as *Ton*, and that's how I will refer to him.

Ton's cousin, Hugh MacKay, was a Gamekeeper at Alisary near Lochailort. Every weekend *Ton* would walk over the mountains from Mingarry to visit him. The route was Mingarry – Kinlochmoidart – Alisary and back on Sunday night. The big attraction was shooting hinds on a Saturday. The rifle used was a .380 calibre, single shot, which one could dismantle, separating the butt from the short barrel. Therefore, stalking, the use of a telescope and shooting started around the age of thirteen.

After attending Church on a Sunday, he, along with a few other boys, would go and locate the army horses which were sheltered in Mingarry wood. The horses were all branded with the letters W.D. (War Department) and the broad arrow army logo. They would ride the horses bareback at the gallop, hanging on to the mane. The horses belonged to Captain Howard, the laird of Dorlin Estate, who commanded the Moidart group of The Lovat Scouts, but no action was ever taken against the boys.

Captain Howard was very fond of my father. When he was winning everything with his rifle shooting, he was to be presented one day with a trophy from the captain, and as he was walking up to receive it, some jealous person shouted out: 'He's good at the deer too,' but Captain Howard never batted an eyelid and said: 'Oh yes, the D, E, A, R.'

Ton was very much influenced by his cousin, Hugh MacKay, and when he left school his cousin thought it would be of benefit to him to go and work for a season on the Ben Alder estate. In those days you weren't a game keeper until you had worked on an estate for five seasons at least, and it was important to get as much experience as you could. Nowadays you can work for one season and get a head keeper's job.

Ton took the boat from Acharacle to Glenfinnan, the train to Roybridge, and he then walked all the way up to the head of Loch Laggan where he was met by a horse and trap which took him the rest of the way to Ben Alder, where he stayed from early August until the middle of October. He then returned home and worked for the winter at the hinds with Hugh MacKay.

3

PRIVATE 1945. JOHN MACDONALD – LOVAT SCOUTS TA

Like many more, *Ton* lied about his age, and enlisted on his 'sixteenth' birthday as a soldier in the Territorial Army, or the 'Terriers' as it was also known. It was a popular choice for many lads in rural areas at this time, as you were required to attend a two-week camp every summer, which eased the monotony of daily life, and you were also paid a small amount, which helped to augment typically poor rural wages. Anything made a difference, when you consider that my father's first wage at Ben Alder was 19 shillings a week.

His unit was 'A' Squadron Lovat Scouts, which had its local drill hall at Shielbridge. 'A' squadron had drill halls in Shielbridge, Fort William, Fort Augustus and Roy Bridge. 1st Lovat Scouts consisted of 4 squadrons – A, B, C and D. The Shielbridge Troop consisted of 22 boys from Moidart and Strontian. Their officer being Captain Howard of Glossop.

They were issued with uniforms straight away – that was part of the attraction – which were their responsibility to look after and maintain in a proper fashion, and they met pretty regularly in the drill hall at Shielbridge for weapons training and drill practice. I don't think they ever engaged in any battle games as such, and they certainly didn't do any work on horseback around here, which is strange when you consider the Army horses that Captain Howard had at his disposal. They were only ever given horses when going to camp, and most of the boys would have been able to ride anyway, and all would have had at least a working knowledge of small arms.

Every year, *Ton* had to attend annual camp at venues like Brodie, Beaufort Castle and Beauly itself, which was the headquarters of the regiment. Being a cavalry regiment, all exercises and training at camp were conducted with horses. There were sports days, shinty matches, highland games and rifle shooting competitions. John was top marksman on two consecutive years at the training camps. It is worth noting that the annual shoot, held every year at Shielbridge shooting range, was also won by John MacDonald from 1910 right up to the summer of 1914. A natural rifle marksman.

Camps lasted for two weeks in the summer months. It must have been quite an occasion going away to camp, and they were allowed to stop at every pub or hotel on the way for a pint of beer – spirits were banned, but pints of beer were allowed. The first stop would be Salen, then Strontian, then Ardgour, where they would get a boat to Fort William.

They would camp there for the night, and then head up Loch Lochy side where they would collect the Fort Augustus boys. Then it was aboard a boat call the Gondolier for the sail up Loch Ness, and they would get off at either Drumnadrochit or Inverness, depending on their final destination.

And if you think that is good, then just remember that they got to stop at every pub for a pint of beer on the way home too.

Now, before you start thinking that this was all one big party, you have to remember that it was usually good weather during those summers long ago, and my father reckoned that half your pint of beer was used for cleaning the stour generated by 100 horses out of your mouth. It is not known whether the Army paid for this generous supply of beer. Camps were also anything but incident free as the next two stories will illustrate.

Iain Mòr a Ruiseanaich was a huge man, with size 11 or 12 feet. They were on their way to camp once, heading up Loch Lochy side when the order was given to give the horses a drink. They always travelled in a particular way. The horses would trot a mile, walk a mile and then the trooper would dismount and walk a mile. That's the way it was and it never changed, with the horses being given a drink every so often too.

The order to give the horses a drink was always given somewhere close to water – in this case Loch Lochy – and you had to dismount immediately and make sure that your horse was catered for, but *Iain Mòr a Ruiseanaich* stayed on his horse against all the rules.

It was possibly the sight of the other horses drinking that caused it, but *Iain Mòr's* horse reared up and slipped down a bank, plunging itself and its rider into the dark depths of the loch.

Troopers were supposed to ride with their toes in the stirrups, but it's reckoned that *Iain Mòr* was in the habit of riding with his big feet right through the stirrup, which made it difficult to break free in the event of an accident. He was most definitely stuck, and no one to this day knows how he managed to get out of that one alive. There must have been a hell of a squabble between *Iain Mòr a Ruiseanaich* and the horse at the bottom of Loch Lochy.

He seemed to stay under for ages, with his comrades on the bank watching nothing but bubbles rising. Sergeant Farrier John MacArthur (*Seonaidh Ghobhainn*) was stripped and ready to jump in when, miraculously, *Iain Mòr* appeared above the surface, without his horse.

The other thing that amazed the boys was that *Iain Mòr's* rifle was strapped around his leg, as that was also one of their rules of transit, but can you imagine the weight that would have added in the water?

There were so many rules broken that day, but there were no recriminations. Captain Howard was just glad that his boys were all safe and well.

Seonaidh Ghobhainn still had to jump in as *Iain Mòr* couldn't swim, but then, *Seonaidh Ghobhainn* was an amazing man. They were heading to camp another year, and there was a horse needing shod – it had been visibly lame going along the road – so they reached the hotel at Strontian where it was decided that everyone else could have a break while *Seonaidh* saw to the horse.

He prepared his kit and got a hold of the horse, which bolted immediately dragging *Seonaidh* behind. He clung on for dear life as the horse galloped on, and he managed to finally get control of her 100 yards out on the foreshore, which is just where he shod her, with all the other troopers looking on amazed. It must have been like the Wild West.

I know that at one of the camps up in Beauly, they did a lot of exercises and mock battles around the Beauly Firth in what must have been a preparation for war.

There was a farmhouse and *Ton* and the boys were told that the enemy were holed up there, and their task was to take the farmhouse back. They were given a particularly nasty stretch of the River Beauly to cross to get to the farmhouse – so bad that when my father eventually got over the river, his saddle was underneath the horse. They had to go right through a salmon pool, which was particularly deep, and they believed that there was a very good reason for why they had been given such a treacherous route.

It was a well-known fact in the ranks that some officers, including Captain Howard, weren't all that popular in the officer's mess. Social status, aristocratic background and religion were the main issues causing disharmony amongst senior and junior officers.

Senior officers at the planning stage of this battle exercise obviously had some issue with Captain Howard, and ordered him and his men to negotiate this treacherous stretch of the river before taking the farmhouse. However, the final outcome resulted in the capture of the farmhouse and prisoners.

Ton and the boys were delighted, but it seems that Captain Howard wasn't congratulated by all his fellow officers.

They were also expected to take part in various different sports at camp. There would be field sports – running, shot put, tug of war – football, shinty and heavy events. The man that always used to win the hammer event was a fellow called Ormiston from Newtonmore, and that family continues their proud sporting heritage to this day.

He must have been a very strong man indeed. All the other boys competing against him were pretty ordinary, and word went round that Ormiston had been competing on the Highland Games circuit. Sure enough, when it came to his turn, he threw the hammer so far that it came through the roof of a tent where the judges were. Luckily, it never hit anybody.

THE GROWING CLAMOUR

It seemed that war was inevitable, and my father could remember things beginning to hot up just before the declaration. Allan MacDonald who worked aboard the steamer Clanranald, that ran a daily service up and down Loch Shiel, had seen two trains full of RNVR sailors, en-route from Lewis and Harris, in Glenfinnan heading south, and word of this spread like wildfire. They had a good idea that the sighting of these 'Blue Jackets' surely meant war.

There was also a green box in the drill hall at Shielbridge that no one was supposed to open or look into, but everyone was only too aware of what was in it. Most importantly, there was a list of names of all the men that lived near the drill hall, and each of these was allotted the name of a man from an outlying area that they would have to go and get in the event of war being declared. Those who lived closest to the hall were actually detailed with checking all the equipment before the other men would return.

On the night of 3rd August 1914, there was a larger than usual gathering of people on the 'new bridge' which crossed the River Shiel. It was a popular place for the young of the area to meet and conduct their courting, but it seems that people of all ages were there that night, attracted by an incredible natural event. Everyone was watching the most spectacular blood red sunset they had ever seen.

A local man, Ronald MacDonald from Moss, who had second sight, predicted a war with fearful bloodshed. No one yet knew of the declaration that was to be made in the Admiralty Building in London the very next day.

Later that evening, *Ton* was getting ready for bed, when his cousin, Corporal Donald MacDonald (*Dòmhnall Raghnall*), came to the house with a mobilisation order and to tell *Ton* that he would have to go to Kinlochmoidart and collect Ronald MacDonald, affectionately known as *Rancan*, a gardener working on the estate. There was no time to lose, *Ton* would have to go immediately and present himself and *Rancan* at Shielbridge Hall by daybreak.

His route would have taken him up through the burn to Mingarry Ard, then over the hill, coming out at the Ard Mollich, before crossing the river and proceeding to Kinlochmoidart House. It's a fair distance, but these guys could shift, even in the dark, and the trip there and back would probably have taken him about three hours.

He was held up after reaching the bothy where *Rancan* was staying, as his comrade refused to believe *Ton* and would not get out of his bed. It took one hour to convince *Rancan* that this was indeed a mobilization order. This reluctance to get out of bed and go to Shielbridge Hall haunted *Ton* for the rest of his life, because, as Highlanders, we are imbued with a sense of the supernatural; we heed warnings and take notice of omens. *Rancan* never returned to Moidart.

Ton and *Rancan* reached the drill hall in the early hours of August 5th. The Moidart troop were all present and correct, and were kitted out with rifle, bayonet and F.S.M.O. – Field Service Marching Order.

At seven in the morning, the Moidart contingent formed up for the roll call on Acharacle Pier. When all were accounted for, they boarded the steamship Clanranald, and sailed up Loch Shiel to Glenfinnan where they marched up to the railway station. (*) There were a number of Boer War veterans in the area at this time who would have understood implicitly what these young men were going through.

The pier at Acharacle, and the railway station at Glenfinnan were crammed full of people. My father said it was more like a festival atmosphere. Spirits were high with excitement and anticipation of what the declaration of war would mean. A lot of whisky was consumed amid dancing, singing, kissing and farewell embraces. Little did anyone realise what the next four years had in store for the revellers. They were on their way to war. *Ton* was twenty-years-old.

* In my own childhood, I can remember Angus MacDonald (*Aonghas Ruadh*) from Dalnabreac as one of the Boer War veterans. *Aonghas Ruadh* had been in the Highland Light Infantry during the war in South Africa, and he was the most fearsome character altogether. He would have been an old man by then, but 'sale day' was still his big day. You would hear him coming home from miles away, singing Gaelic songs at the top of his voice. His sister Bella lived next door to us, and you would see her scurrying to lock her door when she would hear her brother coming. Everyone locked their door when they heard *Aonghas Ruadh* coming. With the drink in, he was still in the Highland Light Infantry shouting: 'Come out, you f**kin' b**tards, I'll kill the lot of you!' at every house he passed. He was a holy terror.

HIGHLAND MOUNTED BRIGADE MOVE TO ENGLAND – 1914

Ton and the Moidart scouts met up with the rest of 'A' Squadron in Fort William and journeyed north to Beauly. There would have been other troops converging on Fort William railway station, but all would have had different destinations. Territorials in the 79th Cameron Highlanders, for example, which accounted for the lion's share of Lochaber's fighting men during the First War, could have been heading to Fort George for basic training.

Towards the end of August, the Scouts were on a troop train heading south for Huntingdon in Cambridgeshire. This meant more battle exercises and teaming up with their friends the Fife and Forfar Yeomanry. Towards the end of November, the scouts were on the move again. This time their destination was a coastal area near Skegness. Their operation was coastal defence guard duties, as there was a possibility of a German landing on that stretch of the coast. Here they remained until once again they were on the move in April 1915. The move took them this time to Hunstanton on the Wash. By this time, the Lovat Scouts were a highly trained cavalry unit. Exercises continued during the summer months, and the boys were on a war footing, expecting to cross the English Channel to France at any time.

However, a change was afoot, as the War Office decided that the Highland Mounted Brigade would become a front line infantry unit, which meant getting rid of their horses. In short, they were no longer an active cavalry brigade, but infantry assault troops. The first the men knew of this was when their horses were taken from them, and it did not go down well. It was a terrible blow to morale.

Two weeks were then spent training the men for infantry warfare. This was intensive training to say the least, with emphasis on rifle shooting and close quarter fighting techniques with bayonet, digging with entrenching spades, attacking trenches, defending trenches and night patrols. The boys knew that active service was on the cards – but where?

The final clue, which confirmed that they would soon be sailing, was the granting of embarkation leave. This would not have been long – just a chance to return home and say a few goodbyes to their nearest and dearest.

After embarkation leave, *Ton* was returning south on a train along with many other scouts, when an incident occurred that could have had serious repercussions. Once again, alcohol played its part. As the train approached the Horseshoe Bend north of Tyndrum, the boys began to see deer on the hillside close to the railway line. Every man was carrying his service rifle, and before anyone could stop them, they had all the windows on the train open, and began blasting at the hapless beasts.

It can be rationalised now as young men letting off steam in a time of great stress, but, as you can imagine, there was hell on. It is impossible to know how many deer were killed, but the land owner was understandably furious at the wanton slaughter, and it took much diplomacy and recompense on the part of the War Office to keep the story out of the press.

LOVAT SCOUTS HEAD FOR THE DARDANELLES WAR ZONE

The Lovat Scouts travelled the breadth of England to Devonport, and, on the 8th September, boarded the Cunard liner Andania, which had been kitted out as a troop ship. Their final destination was Suvla Bay, Gallipoli, but no one aboard knew that as they left the south coast.

Sailing through the Bay of Biscay, the Straits of Gibraltar and on into the Mediterranean, they stopped at Malta for bunkering. I'm not aware that they went ashore, but they had great fun with the Maltese, throwing coins into the water which the locals would dive for.

While sailing passed Gibraltar, *Ton* was standing beside a sergeant from Brae Lochaber who pointed in the direction of Africa and said: 'Oh well, that's where I was at war last,' so even within the squadron, there were still remnants of the Boer War.

They landed at Alexandria for a few days, and then travelled on to the sheltered harbour of Mudros, looking over to Suvla Bay.

Here they saw and heard the horror of war for the first time – shells bursting and lighting up the night sky over Suvla Bay. It must have been a scene from hell. It was there, while watching from the ship's railing, that Sergeant Donald MacDonald – *Dòmhnall Dubh* from Bohuntin in Glen Roy – said to *Ton*, "Bidh tu thall an suid an ath oidhch'." – "You will be over there tomorrow night."

Sure enough, the next night, the Scouts landed at Suvla Bay. Landing craft known as 'beetles' were used for this operation. These craft were jam packed, and my father found himself very near the edge

14

of one of them with no railing to speak of, so he was forced to lean over and grab hold of one of the men standing closer to the centre of the boat, until they hit the beach.

As dawn broke, the Lovat Scouts found themselves in the reserve trenches. Although reserve trenches may have been regarded as relatively safe, they were anything but. The reason being that the Turks had a complete view of the British positions, as they held the higher ground overlooking the area held by our troops.

Ton did not like this particular situation very much. They were busy straight away moving supplies and digging trenches, but this was not to *Ton's* liking. There were a few accidents, like getting hit with a pick or shovel in the backside by one of your own men. Even in the darkness, shells were always bursting with shrapnel flying about the place, as the Turks knew of every movement in the reserve trenches at night. They frequently bombarded the area with heavy and light artillery, as they knew the co-ordinates, having obtained them during daylight hours from their gun crews and observers.

One day, Captain Howard got orders from a senior officer to dig a gun emplacement in broad daylight. This was the height of stupidity as they were in full view of Turkish gun batteries.

The first Turkish salvo was one hundred yards short. The second salvo was fifty yards short. Common sense told them to scatter and dive for shelter in a trench. Sure enough, the next salvo was bang in the centre of where the Moidart boys were digging the gun emplacement. They nearly lost every man. The officer who gave this order in the first place was soon relieved of his duties. *Ton* always maintained that if he and his future partner on the Somme, Willie Boa (*), had been registering for the Turkish gunners, and giving the co-ordinates, the first salvo would have been dead centre of the gun emplacement.

* After Gallipoli, *Ton* joined the newly formed Lovat Scouts Sharp Shooters – L.S.S. They were a unit of snipers and observers operating on the Somme, and Willie Boa was his mate for two years. Snipers operated in pairs.

TON MEETS HIS FIRST TURK

Ton moved into the front-line trenches on 6th October 1915. His first sight of a Turk was at first light on the morning of the 7th. An unarmed Turk came running towards the Lovat Scouts sector of the line. He was a little guy zigzagging across no man's land as fast as his legs would carry him. He was obviously a deserter. The Scouts, together with his friends in the Turkish front line trenches, were all firing at him. It was a miracle that he wasn't killed or wounded. He jumped into the trench bay next to *Ton*, pointing excitedly to his mouth. The boys gave him a handful of hard tack biscuits. *Ton* reckoned that: 'he was munching them like chocolate'. The boys usually broke these biscuits with their bayonets, as they were so hard. The poor chap was then escorted down the line for interrogation.

The Scouts reconnaissance skills were soon put to good use, being sent out into no man's land under cover of darkness to reconnoitre enemy positions. The Turks were out there at night too, though, so it became a bit of a game of cat and mouse, with the opposing factions bumping into each other all the time. Taking prisoners became a big thing, because if you were able to take someone alive, they had to be taken back to your lines immediately for debriefing, which meant an end to your night patrol until the next night.

The size of patrols varied from two to four men. You left your own trench and made your way towards the enemy line. Sometimes this was easier if, for example, a communication trench went closer to the enemy trenches. In some parts of the line, you could be 300 yards from the enemy trenches, and in other parts the distance could be less than 100 yards. It varied an awful lot. In areas where both lines were very close, combatants were able to shout to one another.

One bright, moonlit night, a four-man patrol was on a mission in no man's land, when they came under sniper fire. Suddenly, *Ton* felt a tremor in his rifle. He compared it to someone hitting a fence wire; and one could feel a tremor on a fence wire a good distance away. *Ton* held his rifle up in the moonlight to discover that six inches had been blown off the bayonet. That was the recoil from a bullet that he had felt. How close was that? Eventually the sniper was located up a tree, but the patrol decided not to engage as the Turk had the full advantage of the situation. Light and height were in his favour, and his next shot would have been a kill. So the boys crawled back to the safety of their own lines toot sweet (*) as the Scouts used to say.

Re-entering your own trenches could be problematic too, as there was always a password to be given for that particular night, and sentries were notoriously jumpy about troops returning to their own lines.

A full debrief would then follow with your commanding officer, which, in Gallipoli, meant Captain Howard, and then, if you were lucky, you could find somewhere to get your head down for a few hours. Some of the places the boys had to sleep would beggar belief, but I suppose fatigue would make any corner look comfortable.

You might not be out on patrol the very next night, as there was a rota in place, but if you had a few kills to your name, you could expect to be out all the time, as you were far more use to our side.

The .303 Lee-Enfield rifle was the weapon of choice for the British Army at this time. Patrols were issued with 50 rounds of ammunition, and this rose to 100 rounds if the troops were to be involved in live action, or going over the top. We had an old Lee-Enfield in the house, and I seem to remember that the clips took 5 bullets and you could fit two clips into a magazine.

By the end of the Dardanelles campaign, my father carried two rifles. He carried his usual service rifle, but he also had one wrapped in sacking, which was used for sniping. This weapon had its back and fore sights blackened by a burning candle, so that aiming at targets was easier in snowy conditions. The slightest glint coming off a sight or the barrel could give a sniper's position away, and that could be deadly.

* 'Tout suite' is a corruption of the French phrase *'tout de suite'* – *'all at once,'* and came into popular usage during World War One.

TURKISH SNIPER VERY CLOSE

The nightly routine in a front-line trench bay was one man standing on the fire step, exposed from the waist up, and keeping guard in case of a Turkish attack. The guard was changed every two hours. There were usually four men to each bay. This guard duty was very dangerous, as one can imagine. *Ton* would swipe his hand inches past my face to demonstrate what the draft of a bullet felt like.

On this particular night, Sergeant John Grant from Dalilea, Moidart, who was duty guard sergeant, detailed three men to crawl with him over the parapet and see if they could locate a sniper who was operating very close at hand. There was no reasoning for who was picked, the three men were just chosen at random.

The sniper's game was picking off the silhouette of a soldier on guard duty. For this he had to be very close – which he was. They were crawling, not far out at all from their own trench, when they were aware of a sharp rifle crack around thirty yards in front of them, and John Grant gave the order to stand up and look for the rifle flash from the sniper when he fired next. It must have been incredibly dangerous to expose yourself in this way, but, as all soldiers know, an order is an order. It probably wasn't a very smart thing to do, but how else were they going to get the guy?

Ton told me what happened next. In his own words, he said: 'I can see the flash from the snipers rifle yet. It was to my left. We all saw it clearly and the four of us fired directly into where the flash was. We did not investigate, but there was no more shooting from that position that night. We either got him or he knew we were onto him and decided to get to hell out of it.'

Nobody will ever know if that particular Turkish sniper became yet another fatality, but the actions of the patrol kept him quiet for the rest of that night, or, perhaps, convinced him to move on to another position where he would trouble them no more.

The game of cat and mouse continued, which must have brought its own difficulties. This was no longer a faceless enemy they were fighting, but men whose habits and behaviour they began to recognise and understand. They even gave names to problematic Turkish snipers, which further humanised their foe.

I often think that *Ton* treated the whole thing as a game – a bloody and deadly game, but a game nevertheless. Maybe this was his way of dealing with the chaos and carnage that he saw roundabout him in every waking minute. Maybe that is why these men were picked for the roles they were given, because they could deal with the situation, and were able to bring the fight to the enemy.

SHIEL COTTAGE

Shiel Cottage is on the banks of the river Shiel in Moidart and was home to my father's cousin, Corporal Donald MacDonald, known to all as *Dòmhnall Raghnall*.

Dòmhnall Raghnall shared a four-man bay in the front line trench with three other Moidart boys: Ronald MacDonald (*Rancan*) from Langal, John MacDonald (*Ton*) from Mingarry and Charlie MacDonald (*Tearlach Mhìcheal*) from Dorlin. The boys named their bay 'Shiel Cottage,' and had it printed on a slab of wood. Now and again, a Serpent would poke its head out of a hole in the bank beside them, have a look around and then retreat back to its nest.

I suppose the 'Shiel Cottage' sign would have been a bit of light relief for them, and a reminder of home when it was needed most. It must be remembered that there were long periods of inactivity, which meant terrible boredom, and that could be just as dangerous as Turkish shells or bullets. It became hard to keep men primed and vigilant during these times, and you were more likely to let your guard down.

One of the games they would play to alleviate the boredom involved a trenching spade, which would be waved above the parapet of the British trench. This was to wake up any alert Turkish snipers. The boys would then attach the trenching spade to a longer bit of wood and wave it above the parapet once again. This time, there would be a 'ping' almost immediately, as the Turkish sniper hit the spade dead centre – something that they managed almost every time.

My father reckoned that the Turks were such good snipers because, just like themselves, many of them were country boys from mountainous areas. They too had grown up using guns in rough terrain, so were every bit as effective a sniping unit in Gallipoli as the Lovat Scouts. Many of the Turks were shepherds and hunters just like their counterparts in the British trenches, and if you had experience of using a fairly basic rifle in everyday life, then firing a military issue weapon must have seemed like the easiest thing on earth.

There was a definite respect between the two sides, and *Ton* always said that the Turks were just boys like himself that had been put there by idiots too, and he never referred to the Germans as the enemy either.

Another favourite pass time for the Scouts was shooting at migrating geese in their V formation flying high above the trenches. Indeed, this was a sport that both British and Turkish front line troops could enjoy. The bullets must have been close, as *Ton* could see the geese weaving and diving high up in the sky as thousands of bullets whizzed by them. I don't suppose many, if any, of these geese were ever eaten, but then, if a goose were to fall in no man's land, I wouldn't want to be the guy that goes and recovers it. You would be the goose very shortly!

It wasn't considered a waste of ammunition as they were blasting away at things all the time, and the officers were quite encouraging of anything that helped to keep your eye in. The Turks, for example, had a white horse that the Scouts could see almost a mile away from the Turkish front line, and they were forever firing at that poor creature, though I'm not sure they ever hit it.

'PERCY' – THE TURKISH SNIPING ACE

Percy, as the Lovat Scouts named him, was a particularly difficult adversary. He was also just about the best sniper that the Turks had on their side. He was notorious amongst the British troops, not just because of his prowess with the trenching spade, but because of the number of kills he was reckoned to have had to his name.

One day, *Ton* was in the second line with a mixture of Lovat Scouts and Fife and Forfars. He recalled this boy washing his shirt and hanging it on a bush to dry. He was a Glasgow lad called Bogie, from the Fife and Forfars. *Ton* told him to be careful going out to collect the shirt when it dried, even though they were behind the front-line trench.

'Bogie jumped out of the trench and was taking his shirt off the bush. He shouted, "Oh," clutching his shirt in one hand, with his other hand above his head as he dropped to the ground. Bogie was later recovered with a bullet through his chest and another bullet through the palm of the hand that was above his head as he dropped to the ground.'

Percy was credited with that kill, which must have been at quite a range, and fast. Remember, this happened in the reserve second line.

The order finally came to get rid of him, and the task was given to the Lovat Scouts. They pretty well knew the location he was operating in, as there had been a lot of damage done there, so a platoon was dispatched to find him, and, if necessary, kill him. This was a night-time operation too.

The attack went in, with *Ton* in the reserve wave waiting on a Very light signal to join the assault, but he didn't go over the top, as the signal never came. *Percy* was located in a sniper's hide in no man's land, and, as per usual, there were two of them. *Percy* was shot dead by Corporal Angus MacKay from Sutherland at very close quarters. However, Corporal MacKay received a bayonet wound from *Percy's* mate, which put him out of action. *Percy's* mate was shot dead by another Lovat Scout in Corporal MacKay's section. The stretcher-bearers then brought Corporal MacKay back to the Lovat Scouts front line position, and then to the casualty clearing area that they had named 'Perth Station.'

'Corporal MacKay passed me, lying wounded on the stretcher. He said: "Fhuair mi e!" – "I got him!"'

Even in the trenches, the method of communication favoured by all these boys was their Gaelic language.

Ton recalled seeing *Percy's* rifle strapped to Corporal MacKay's stretcher with a ticket on it, and he often wondered what happened to it afterwards. It could be somewhere in Sutherland to this day.

The most chilling aspect of this is that when they eventually found *Percy* he had numerous British dog tags round his neck.

STORY OF THE BELT

One night *Ton* was at his post in the front line. A party of four scouts appeared from a communication trench and were passing through *Ton's* position en route to no man's land on a mission. It was a very cold frosty night. One of the party, Charlie MacDonald (*Tearlach Mhìcheal*), recognized *Ton* in the darkness and said: 'I've lost my belt, can I borrow yours to wrap around my great coat?' *Ton* gave him his belt without question, and remembered saying: 'see you in the morning. Good luck.'

At dawn, after giving the code word to the sentry to re-enter their lines, all four jumped back into the trench with a Turkish prisoner. *Ton* immediately asked for his belt back. Now, Charlie MacDonald had been in *Ton's* class at Mingarry School and both were great friends. *Ton* noticed that the front of Charlie's coat was in tatters, and asked him: 'where's my belt?' Charlie handed back the belt, which was only half the length it should have been, with no buckle. A bullet had blown the buckle clean away, leaving Charlie without so much as a scratch on him. You just don't get much closer than that. My father and *Tearlach Mhìcheal* must have discussed that belt many a time – wouldn't they just? –

After the war, *Tearlach Mhìcheal* returned home and worked as a gardener at Dorlin. The estate was a big employer and many of the men were gardeners. Sadly, he died young.

By this time, *Ton* was a Postman and was in the habit of getting a cup of tea from Charlie's sister Mary Ann, who lived alone in Dorlin. *Ton* was shown the remains of that belt on a number of occasions, and often commented that something should be done about it, as, one day, nobody would know the significance of it, but everyone was so busy with their own lives that nothing was ever done.

When Mary Ann passed away, some young family members came to clear the house, and, not knowing the history of this old bit of belt lying in a drawer, they threw it on a bonfire. How terribly sad.

There were a lot of near ones in Gallipoli. There was a man from Morar serving with *Ton*. He was having his breakfast one morning – whatever that amounted to – when he was hit in the head by a stray bullet. It entered at his forehead and followed the line of his skull, exiting at the back of his head. You see, a bullet is a sharp thing, and if it gets the least encouragement at all, it will follow a line. Miraculously, that man survived, but had a plate inserted in his head, and spent the rest of his life in a care home. He would come home to Morar for two weeks every year, accompanied by a nurse.

RONALD MACDONALD – RANCAN

This was a night that came back to haunt my father for the rest of his life. Sergeant John Grant was duty N.C.O. in charge of the section of the line, which included 'Shiel Cottage'. Sergeant Grant would change the guards in this section every two hours. The guard on duty would jump up on the fire step, on watch in case of an attack. This would mean being totally exposed from the chest upward with your rifle at the ready. This was the routine for those left behind in the frontline trench every evening from dusk to dawn.

There were flakes of snow in the air and a severe frost, and *Ton* was first on watch. Sergeant Grant was doing his rounds and gave the order to change guard, so *Ton* jumped down and *Rancan* jumped up on the fire step and took his position. *Ton* reckoned it was only a matter of seconds before *Rancan* came crashing down from the fire step and landed at the bottom of the trench stone dead. The bullet passed straight through his neck.

'I had never witnessed so much blood.'

The Turkish sniper was reckoned to have been very close. A Shell burst or Very light just behind the front line would silhouette a range of targets to choose from.

Rancan had been a school friend – most of them were in 'Shiel Cottage' – so you can imagine just how profound an effect his death had on all the boys. He was buried later that night in what was called 'Shrapnel Valley.'

Ton talked about this tragic event for the rest of his life, always referring to the mobilisation night when *Rancan* would not wake up and had to be physically pulled out from his bed, never to return to Moidart. He often said that *Rancan* should never have gone to war; he wasn't supposed to get out of his bed on the night that *Ton* had gone for him; it wasn't his time. He often wondered if *Rancan* had some inkling of the fate that awaited him.

My father reckoned that the boys who were there divided into two camps. There were those who prayed constantly for deliverance, and there were those who firmly believed that it wouldn't happen to them. I think my father was very much in the second camp; more so when he was over in France. He came through the whole thing without a scratch, and seemed to know that that was the way it would be.

It seems that the one time everyone was united in worrying for their safety was when there was a big attack on and they were expected to go over the top. Everyone knew that the second you put your nose over that parapet, you could be mowed down by machine gun fire. The chances of survival were slim then. You look at the 1st July 1916 in the sector of the Somme where they went over. 60,000 casualties? These boys knew that their luck was zero.

LOCHIEL'S VICTORY AT LOOS.

The Lovat Scouts knew little or nothing about how the war was progressing on the Western Front. They had enough to contend with in their own theatre of war in Gallipoli, fighting the Turks. Anyway, a stern reminder of events in France was to cause alarm and confusion on a scale never witnessed by the Lovat Scouts since they had landed at Suvla Bay.

On a cold frosty night in October, word was passed along the line that on the stroke of midnight, every man had to give three cheers for 'Lochiel's great victory at the battle of Loos.' You see, the Lovat Scouts and Cameron Highlanders drew the majority of their men from the County of Inverness-shire, especially the Lochaber area.

At Loos, the 5th Battalion Queens own Cameron Highlanders, commanded by Colonel Donald Cameron of Lochiel went into action on 25th September 1915 with a battalion strength of 820 officers and men. At roll call after the action, the battalion strength amounted to around 160. The casualty rate was horrendous, given the stupidity of those in command and the unquestioned bravery of the men, with Corporal Pollock being awarded the V.C.

At midnight on the dot, three massive cheers went up right along the trenches in Gallipoli. 'Johnnie Turk,' as the Lovat Scouts called their nemesis, opened up with everything he had – heavy artillery, rifle and machine gun fire and Very lights of every colour in the rainbow. The bombardment was horrific, with the main barrage focused on the forward front line positions. So concentrated was the barrage that, in *Ton's* own words: 'you could read the Oban Times in the front line trench.'

You see, the three cheers at midnight caused panic in the Turkish lines, as they thought that our boys were going over the top on a full-scale night attack and assault on their lines. I wonder if Lochiel ever knew about the frightening incident caused by the order given to celebrate his victory.

In hindsight, it seems unbelievable that an order of this sort would be given, drawing attention to the British front lines, but I suppose these were extraordinary circumstances. It reminds me of what my father said about the Anzacs. He thought they were stone mad. They used to sing songs round campfires at night, and the next minute the Turks would send a shell in on top of them. It was so easy for them. Their revelry and the fires would give their positions away completely. It was terribly dangerous behaviour, but that was the way the Australians and the New Zealanders were.

Ton and the rest of the boys had, of course, no idea of the casualties suffered by the Camerons at Loos. It may not have been until after the war that the true extent of the slaughter was made public, as these things were always kept quiet for the sake of morale. The people of Lochaber were up in arms when they did eventually find out.

Luckily for the Scouts, the Turkish bombardment that night didn't cause significant damage; for once.

ENCOUNTER WITH THE GHURKHAS

During October *Ton* began to put his shooting skills to good use. Officers and N.C.O's took note of this guy, recommending a special .303 rifle for him. He was then detailed for many night operations in no man's land, coupled with the usual daylight sniping and shooting at long range. As you now know, the back and fore sights were burned with a lit candle until they became black, which not only cut down on glare, but made it easier to focus on a target in white frost and snowy conditions.

One night, he was on a special mission with Corporal Donald MacDonald (*Dòmhnall Raghnall*) out in no man's land. For some reason, they were lying low in a shell hole pretty near the Turkish front line. All of a sudden, three men jumped into the shell hole along with them and began talking in a foreign language. *Dòmhnall Raghnall* turned to *Ton*, and said: 'we're f****d now, *Ton*.'

It turned out that the guys sharing the shell hole were Ghurkhas, armed with nothing but their famous khukuri knives, and so began a lengthy conversation in sign language. *Ton* and Donald wanted to see their knives, but the Ghurkhas would not show them – there may have been some sacred reason for this. The Ghurkhas made a gesture of cutting someone's throat accompanied by a gurgling sort of sound. *Ton* remembered seeing them crawl out of the shell hole, flat on their bellies like snakes, heading in the direction of the Turkish forward positions. Little did the Turks know what was heading their way. *Ton* reckoned they were the best in the business.

WEATHER BREAKS – HELL UPON EARTH.

After two to three weeks out of the action, the Lovat Scouts were ordered back up the line towards the end of November. From 26th November up to early December, the Dardanelles experienced the worst weather conditions witnessed in the region for over fifty years. It started with a torrential downpour of rain and sleet, followed by a blizzard, and finished up with temperatures well below zero. Under these conditions, the Lovat Scouts took over the front-line trenches only to find these, the reserve trenches and communication trenches flooded due to floodwater bursting the barricades in the riverbed. The Turkish trenches were also flooded waist deep.

One morning as dawn broke, directly opposite *Ton's* forward position, the Turks were seen to be jumping out of their flooded trenches. *Ton* got two or three sand bags in place above the parapet and started shooting at targets around the 200 yards range. He was also picking off targets in the Turkish reserve trench areas that were also flooded. *Ton* never gave me any indication of how many. Nevertheless, Moidart boys who witnessed this solo shoot out had their own numbers documented in their minds and talked about them for many years. Donald MacLean, the local Postman, told me once what the figures were, but I don't think it would be right to repeat it. He was watching the whole affair along with Sergeant John Grant and *Dòmhnall Raghnall*. Donald said: 'none of us were shooting, as our fingers were almost frozen stiff with the cold.' *Ton* more than made up for them. As Donald MacLean told me: 'He emptied his magazine over and over again. It was like shooting hinds on a winter's morning,' which paints a horrifying picture, and not one that anyone can be proud of, but that is the dreadful reality of war, and who are we, who were not there, to judge?

The following morning a group of Turks were observed sitting in a row above the parapet, in a reserve trench about 300yards out – a safe distance. As my father said: 'the first one keeled over. They must have thought it was a stray bullet. The next one keeled over – another stray bullet. When the third one keeled over, someone must have locked onto the fact that these were not stray bullets. Like a flash, they all jumped up and dived into the trench out of sight.'

Once again, *Ton's* shooting skills, if that's what one can call it, were noted by his officers and documented.

During the first few days in December Ton was credited with other isolated sniping missions in no man's land, mainly picking off targets at close range.

POSTING THE GUARD.

During the terrifying few days of rain, flooding, snow and severe frost, the battle continued as usual. The section of the line where 'A' squadron were positioned was a total shambles. The firing line trench had collapsed, including the parapet, leaving the Scouts very exposed to shelling and sniper fire. Standing up was very dangerous.

One night, the guard commander, who was responsible for posting his section of men at various points and changing the guard every two hours, somehow did not change guard number twelve at his post. The poor man left at his post was Donald MacLean. Before dawn, this terrible mistake was discovered, with Donald stiff as a poker and suffering severe hypothermia. Ton spoke about this unfortunate incident a lot, and wondered why Donald MacLean was not recommended for a Military Medal for staying at his post. Donald was taken back to base that day, suffering severe frostbite, and evacuated back to Alexandria.

I've often wondered what was going through his head as the hours ticked by and he still wasn't being relieved. It was a terrible mistake that could have had the worst consequences.

Donald was a lovely man. He lost a finger in Salonika. They made him into a machine gunner after Gallipoli, and he found himself in action one day when, all of a sudden, his gun jammed. He tried to free the blockage in the breech, and the ammunition belt began moving again and took his finger with it.

No 8 Group, Snipers Selection Training Course – Beauly, early 1917.

No 8 Group. Only 20 were awarded the coveted LSS Badge.

John MacDonald and Willie Boa – Sniper pair operating on the Western Front, Somme Sector, 1917 and 1918.

Captain John MacGillivray – No. 8 Group, Lovat Scouts Sharpshooters

The MacGillivrays of Calrossie – Duncan, world champion piper and grandson of Captain John, and Duncan's son Iain, Commander of Clan MacGillivray and great-grandson of Captain John.

Captain John MacGillivray's Ross telescope.

Captain John MacGillivray with one of his famous pedigree shorthorn bulls.

Donald Cameron of Lochiel – commanding officer Lovat Scouts Sharpshooters 1917 /18.

Lord Lovat – commanding officer of the
Lovat Scouts in Gallipoli.

Padre Rev. Hugh Cameron, Suvla Bay,
Gallipoli.

The author, Fergie MacDonald – musician.

The author, Fergie MacDonald – National Service Physical Training Instructor, Aldershot 1955.

Captain Lord Howard, Moidart Group – A Squadron.

Moidart and Strontian Lovat Scouts at the TA Annual camp, July 1914. John '*Ton*' MacDonald is on the extreme left, front row.

John 'Ton' MacDonald's 'Dog Tag' worn during 1917 and 1918 on the Western Front – 'MacDonald J126315 LSS.'

'He died for king and country…' – Memorial plaque presented to the family of Ronald MacDonald, killed at Suvla Bay, Gallipoli, 1915.

John 'Ton' MacDonald, postman 1921 to 1960 – delivering mail by boat to Eilean Shona.

John '*Ton*' MacDonald aged 90 fishing on Loch Shiel.

A good days fishing – The March Pool, Kinlochmoidart River 1983.

John F. MacDonald following in his grandfather's footsteps – British Olympic Trap Shooting Champion 2014. John has represented Great Britain at World and European Championships and Commonwealth Games.

Christmas and New Year card, December 1918.

John *Ton* MacDonald and Mima, Mingarry 1980. My mother often said: 'I could walk to the Dardanelles and back blindfolded.'

John MacDonald (Fergie's son) shooting for Scotland.

PADRE FATHER HUGH CAMERON – ROY BRIDGE.

'I remember one morning in freezing conditions, with the forward firing line trench blown to bits, meeting Father Hugh Cameron who was administrating communion. He was crawling on his knees and giving communion to boys lying on their bellies or crouched up because of deadly Turkish sniper fire.'

Ton always talked about this padre, Father Hugh Cameron, who shared, without hesitation, all the dangers, whether front line or reserve trenches, along with his boys. He was an extremely brave man, who thought nothing of putting his own life on the line.

He was from Roy Bridge, and went to Gallipoli with the Lovat Scouts in 1915. His war diary has just recently been published, and is a wonderful account of the conditions faced by all ranks during the war.

It must have been so important for morale to have Father Hugh on hand to celebrate mass, take confession and administer last rites to the sick and dying. The old maxim that there are no atheists in foxholes would have, I'm sure, held true.

My father was a practising Catholic, although very middle of the road in his views, after all, my mother was a strict Presbyterian from Morvern, but I'm sure he would have been comforted greatly by Father Hugh's presence.

DONALD JOHN IS TAKEN PRISONER

When the weather cleared up after the floods and snow, the days were clear but bitterly cold and freezing. *Ton* was in a sniping position in no man's land along with another boy, trying to pick off targets, when, to their astonishment, they spotted two Lovat Scouts walking straight into the Turkish forward trenches. *Ton* recognized one of them, Donald John (*Domhnall Iain*) from South Uist.

'I saw *Domhnall Iain* and another Scout carrying pots and walking straight into a Turkish front-line position. I shouted to them to come back, they stopped, turned round and made an effort to turn back, but then they walked forward and disappeared into the forward Turkish trench.'

Ton was always sure that the 'Dixies' (pots) were full of soup or water for the Lovat Scout forward front-line positions. The boys must have got confused in a communication trench, and came face-to-face with a Turk in a forward position of his own, with a rifle and indicating to them to come forward. Donald John died in Turkey as a Prisoner of War.

The layperson's impression of a trench is that it is a straight line, but it is anything but. The line changed so often on both sides that it became very hard to know exactly where you were, and, at times, whether you were actually in a friendly trench. The worst job my father ever had was in France, where the Lovat Scouts Sharp Shooters were expected to report on positions of the enemy lines and the depth of their barbed wire defences. It became so difficult to know where you were or where you were going that my father often expected to be cut off from his comrades in an instant. He could sympathise completely with the plight of poor Donald John.

It must have been a dreadful moment to realise that in the blink of an eye the game was up and you were suddenly a Turkish prisoner. They must have wandered into an old communication trench and became victims of the ever-changing line. They were reckoned to be the only two Lovat Scouts taken prisoner in the Dardanelles campaign.

A GENTLEMAN'S WAR?

Ton recalled being on a four-man night patrol in no man's land and capturing a Turkish sniper during the action. The sniper's mate was not so lucky and was killed at close quarters, so the patrol got back to the British trenches and waited for escorts to take the prisoner down the line for interrogation.

The captured prisoner's rifle was of great interest to the boys, but someone noticed that, for some unknown reason, it had not been fired. However, on further inspection the bullet that was 'up the shoot' was what was known as a 'dumdum' – designed to expand on impact for maximum damage. The rest of the bullets in the magazine were all legal and sharp-pointed.

Ton said that this was normal practise when occupying frontline positions. The first bullet would be filed and doctored, as this would most certainly be a kill. This establishes the fact that both sides were at it, and were breaking the Hague Convention of 1899, Declaration III, which banned the use of such bullets in warfare, but I suppose anything goes on a battlefield when the object of the exercise is to kill the enemy.

On a lighter note, I remember when I was about nine-years-old there was a stag jumping our fence every night and eating our corn. My father had hundreds of army issue .303 bullets, and one evening I saw him filing one down and engraving an 'X' on the flattened head, and he explained why. The stag was shot between the eyes, as one would expect from a sniper, and I shall never forget the exit wound the bullet created.

It was years after that he told me of the use of dumdum bullets in Gallipoli, and I immediately thought of the stag and shuddered!

REARGUARD ACTION – EVACUATION AND GOODBYE GALLIPOLI

Apart from dead and wounded casualties, a large number of Lovat Scouts went down with dysentery. Many had to be taken out of the line, but *Ton* was fortunate not to go down with this terrible illness. Lord Lovat himself was invalided out of the trenches because of it, and it is said that he never got over it.

Plans to evacuate the troops away from this disaster began around the 10th December. During the final days of the evacuation, the Lovat Scouts and Ghurkhas were sacrificed, or, shall we say, got the honour of fighting a rearguard action. This enabled the thousands of troops at Suvla Bay to carry out a nightly evacuation, reaching the beaches undetected and boarding boats to reach the safety of Mudros. On the 20th December, the small party of Lovat Scouts and Ghurkhas eventually left the beaches of Suvla Bay where they had landed three months earlier.

'I volunteered to be the last man evacuated from Suvla Bay. There was an unofficial lottery among the boys, but my name did not come out of the hat.'

The subterfuge involved to conceal the evacuation was incredible. There were rifles rigged to fire on their own all along the British front line to give the impression that the British troops were still there.

Did the Turks know? *Ton* reckoned they did, but decided not to attack. General Sir Charles Monro, the British general who carried out the massive evacuation, did so with unquestioned military brilliance, and it would be fair to say that he was the only British commander to come out of this disaster with any credibility, but one incident in particular convinced my father that 'Johnnie Turk' knew exactly what was going on.

On the final night of the evacuation of Suvla Bay, *Ton* was on board one of the last small crafts pulling away from the shore when figures were spotted on the beach gesturing and shouting for a boat to come back. The officers on board were not comfortable with this, as the shadowy figures had been identified as Turks.

The Turks did not open fire as they might have done, but ushered an allied prisoner forward, who was able to wade out to the safety of the boat and his comrades without a shot being fired. The story went round that the British prisoner was held captive until the evacuation took place. Ton reckoned that this incident was a final act of defiance by the Turks; a way of saying: "we know what you are up to." Either way, the prisoner, I am sure, couldn't believe his luck.

This first hand account challenges previously held beliefs that the subterfuge had worked, but does not diminish the fact that the evacuation was itself a huge success at the end of a disastrous military campaign.

EGYPT

At the end of December, *Ton* arrived in Alexandria. Can you imagine the Lovat Scouts coming from the hellish battle zone of Gallipoli and camping for a rest period there? It is the only time in my life that I ever doubted my father's integrity. He told me often, 'I was the only man in 'A' Squadron who didn't frequent the parlours and brothels of Sister Street.' Then again, maybe that's correct, as he always spoke poorly of the boys on sick parade with a 'dose.' He didn't like that, and I don't blame him.

The boys were there for a month, and I'm sure there would have been some stories told after that. Can you just imagine? It wasn't just the Lovat Scouts, of course. There were many other soldiers there as well of all different nationalities. Some would be going home, and some would be shipping out to other theatres of war, but all were there for their hard earned rest and recuperation.

There were other ways to relax too if Sister Street wasn't to your fancy. I know that they did a lot of going round looking for souvenirs, for example. It must have seemed such a strange world to them. They had come from a place where they were face-to-face with death every day, and now here they were in this metropolis with all its new sights and sounds and smells, where no one was trying to kill you.

EGYPT – THE DESERT-DISCHARGE

In February 1916, the Lovat Scouts moved out of Alexandria into the desert to guard areas that were under threat from raiding desert tribesmen.

Ton recalled buying oranges by the dozen and squeezing the juice out of them one by one to quench his thirst. The desert heat was almost unbearable, reaching temperatures of up to 120 degrees Fahrenheit. The friendly Arabs had a field day selling oranges and anything else they could get their hands on. Interestingly enough, *Ton* had in his possession, for many years, two 12-bore cartridges with a broad arrow and the letters WD inscribed on them. Sometimes when guarding the camp at night, the Lovat Scouts were issued with shotguns, along with their rifles, of course, but, on the whole, the Scouts got on really well with the local Desert Arabs.

While on these desert operations in the sweltering heat, someone told him that his name was up in orders and to report to the commanding officer in the morning. He duly reported and, being a time expired territorial soldier, he was given the option to sign on and remain with the battalion in Egypt or get shipped back to Scotland and re-enlist for further army service. However, the officer was aware of a new specialized unit being formed up in Beauly, comprised of snipers and observers, training for special operations on the Western Front. They were called the Lovat Scouts Sharpshooters, or LSS for short.

This appealed to *Ton*, and the officer recommended on his discharge papers that 1945 Private John MacDonald was a suitable candidate to enrol on this very special course because of his exploits as a battalion sniper in Gallipoli. *Ton* was on his way.

He was allowed home for a few months, which must have been a great boon, and he was even able to hold down a bit of work here and there while waiting to receive his orders to begin training for the Sharp Shooters.

This was probably a bit of an oversight on the part of the War Office, as the recruiting sergeants scouring the Highlands at that time for new recruits and conscription dodgers didn't seem to have any idea that he had returned home. The NCO that travelled around Moidart and Ardnamurchan went by the name of Sergeant Lottie. He must have had his own section area, and he would come round looking for known dodgers that had gone to ground. He was a notorious character at that time, and was known to approach any young man of fighting age and enquire why they weren't away fighting for king and country. If you couldn't give him a good reason why you hadn't been called up, you would be in hot water.

BEAULY – LOVAT SCOUTS SHARPSHOOTERS – L.S.S.

I'm not sure if things had got hot for *Ton*, but in early 1917 he re-enlisted at the Cameron Barracks, Inverness, with an excellent report on his discharge papers, giving reference to sniping in Gallipoli, and an accompanying letter from his commanding officer. This meant he would not have to do basic training again like the raw recruits who were enlisting for the first time. He counted himself very, very lucky, because without those papers he would have been sent to the Cameron Highlanders and straight to the frontline in France, where his prospects would have been bleak.

He was ordered to report to the Lovat Scouts Sharpshooters' headquarters in Beauly, but would have to wait three weeks for the next training intake. A group started with around 50 men on each course – not all of whom had seen action – and then, finally, the group was trimmed down to 20 men. Only the elite and very best got presented with the distinguished Lovat Scouts Sharpshooters' insignia 'LSS,' which they wore with pride and honour.

Each group of twenty snipers was commanded by one officer. The Officer assigned to No 8 group was Captain John MacGillivray of Calrossie in Easter Ross.

Although the majority of this special unit were stalkers and gamekeepers, the group would be made up to full strength by drafting in specially selected men from other infantry units; mainly Highland regiments. If they did not make the grade, they would be returned to their respective units immediately.

The course was difficult and intense. Heavy emphasis was put on telescope techniques for observing objects of up to 10-miles in range;

often having to identify the name and number of fishing boats going through the Caledonian Canal. Pass marks had to be obtained in shooting, ballistics, wind adjustment, map reading and accurate reading of enemy positions using protractor and compass in order to give a map reference. In short, a working knowledge of geometry and trigonometry were most important, and it always amazed me that a man like my father, who had very little schooling at all, was able to talk on these subjects with great authority.

Ton got his 'cross guns' and an extra one shilling per week. Gaining your 'cross guns' meant seven hits on the 'running man' target at 300 yards for the ordinary infantry soldier, and ten for a sniper. Ton got thirteen hits out of fifteen, and was very proud of that.

From day one on the sniper's course, each man was paired with another at random. *Ton* was paired with Willie Boa from Glen Affric. They remained a pair during the war on the Somme and the Western Front, and remained close friends after the war for the rest of their lives. Willie Boa was a rookie at this point, not having served before, but they must have hit it off immediately. I suppose they had so much in common, given their mutual love of deer and the hills.

The course lasted roughly 8 to 10 weeks, which would have given them ample time to get acquainted. There was a lot to learn in that short time, and your focus had to be complete, with continual assessment a part of the daily routine. The standards were extremely high and you had to come up to the mark, but if you gave of your best and managed to stay the course, you would be presented with your LSS badges – which were worn on the shoulder – at a passing out parade in Beauly.

LSS No 8 GROUP POSTED TO THE SOMME

The draft left Inverness Railway Station in May 1917 – 20 snipers under Captain John MacGillivray, including 126315 John McDonald LSS. Only 9 groups of this elite unit ever served in France. Each group was assigned to a corps. Ton's No 8 group were attached to 1st Corps operating in the Bapaume, Cambrai and St Quentin sector, on the Somme front. Ton's arrival coincided with a change in command. Colonel Donald Cameron of Lochiel took over from Lord Lovat and commanded the Lovat Scouts Sharpshooters until the end of the war.

The sharpshooters were the eyes of their corps headquarters. Their main task was locating German heavy gun batteries, and feeding the information to Captain John MacGillivray, who then relayed the co-ordinates to the heavy corps artillery batteries behind the British lines. Watches would be synchronized, and at a given time, salvos from the 'corps heavies' as the snipers called them, would bombard these German gun battery emplacements. While this bombardment was going on, the two or sometimes four snipers involved in the particular operation would monitor the action, and relay this information back to Captain MacGillivray also, who, in turn, kept the artillery battery officer informed of the situation.

Concentrated troop movements reinforcing sections of the German front line, indicating an attack, were observed and dealt with in the same manner, and news of the Lovat Scouts Sharpshooters' participation on the Somme front soon filtered through to the German high command. The skills of this elite unit were reeking havoc on the German divisions in forward and rear positions of their lines.

Ton's diary from this time reads: 'One day a German aeroplane appeared and dropped thousands of pamphlets from the sky. The heading on the pamphlet had the Lovat Scouts Sharpshooters logo printed at the top i.e. "LSS" The message was brief and to the point and read "Any LSS sniper captured will not be treated as a prisoner of war but torn to pieces and shot."' From then on, Captain John MacGillivray made it crystal clear that none of his boys in No 8 group. LSS were ever to get captured, and none of them ever did.

They often bumped into German patrols when out in no man's land, but they were told to get the hell out of there and never put themselves in a situation that could result in capture.

By and large, though, conditions were better for the LSS boys than they had been in Gallipoli. For one, they were billeted well behind their own lines, where the only real danger to them was shellfire. It was certainly better than being canon fodder in a frontline trench with, say, the Seaforths or Camerons. They had far more control over their own safety than ordinary frontline infantry, in as much as they could spot danger and react to it as they saw fit, rather than the poor boys that were just ordered over the top on the whim of a battalion commander.

They were busy with missions, of course, but as the whole point of these was to stay hidden and concealed, the odds of you coming home alive were much more in your own hands. You relied more upon your own judgement. Their intelligence work had to be spot on, and coordinates given had to be completely accurate, but they had all been selected because they were well capable of delivering results.

You must remember that it wasn't just the artillery that relied upon their intelligence work. Those self same guys in the Seaforths and Camerons were just as reliant on them. When you went over the top, you had to know exactly where you were going and who you were attacking. Intelligence gathered from their own lines was at best patchy, so they needed the LSS boys venturing into no man's land night after night to be able to build up a better idea of the enemy they were facing.

The Somme was a dreadful theatre of war – easily as bad as anything that *Ton* had seen in Gallipoli – but it is incredible just how resilient humans can be in the face of terrible adversity. Men still looked for distractions and ways to take their minds off the terrible slaughter around them. There was even a lovely looking French girl, who the boys nicknamed *Cailleach Cliathraidh*, that seemed to frequent the frontline on an almost daily basis. *Ton* could never understand how she got away with selling here wares, as it were.

DANGEROUS ASSIGNMENTS – JOHN MACHARDY

Ton and Willie Boa were on a mission in a snipers hideout in no man's land. Avoiding detection in this den was imperative, especially entering and leaving. After 48 hours in this position, they were relieved by another two snipers; John MacHardy from Knoydart and Mathieson from Kinlochleven. *Ton* and Willie Boa were not all that long back in their billet, well behind the lines, when who walked in but MacHardy and Mathieson. Captain MacGillivray was furious, enquiring as to why they had left their post. Now, as a point of interest, the snipers always wore their Balmoral bonnets, which had black and white dicing round the bottom and a toorie sitting on top, but, when on a mission, this distinctive bonnet was covered with a khaki coloured camouflage veil.

'John MacHardy threw his bonnet, or what was left of it, on the table and just said "look." The German sniper's bullet had made a trench right along the top of the Balmoral, and had blown the toorie clean away.'

The pair of them had been detected and tracked by a pair of German snipers.

'The next bullet would have been through the forehead as they were just as good at shooting as our boys were.'

Ton had the greatest respect for his opposite numbers in the German infantry. He would never hear a bad word against them.

'It was time for MacHardy and Mathieson to tout suite.'

John MacHardy was head keeper over in Knoydart for many years, and, one day, Louis Stewart and Iain MacKay from the Red Deer

Commission were tasked with going over there to deal with a problem. It seems that there were deer marauding into a field, and the landowner wanted to shoot them – or at least their leader.

After they had had a quick cup of tea, Louis Stewart wanted to know where the deer to be dealt with were, so John MacHardy took him directly to the spot, which was up a hill somewhere.

They got their telescopes out and could see the deer sunning themselves quite happily on a slope below them, so Louis Stewart turned to Iain MacKay and suggested that they get closer to the beasts. Now, Louis Stewart was a crack shot international shooter with 25 Scotland caps to his name, so you can imagine John MacHardy – who was an old man by then – looking amazed at such a suggestion. The old sniper was appalled that the headman from the Red Deer Commission couldn't shoot them from that range. 'Are you not going to shoot them from here?' he asked. That shows you just how good the Lovat Scouts Sharp Shooters were.

URQUHART

Urquhart had been drafted into the Lovat Scouts Sharpshooters from another unit. During the retreat, they were sitting by a roadside when they saw a group of captured Germans being taken away to the rear. As they were going by, Urquhart jumped out and grabbed a hold of one of the Germans and indicated that he wanted to see the man's hand.

He had spotted a ring that the poor German was wearing, and began yanking at his finger to get it off, but it must have been tight and wouldn't budge. He turned to my father and shouted: 'Give me your knife, John,' but my father refused.

He had never liked Urquhart anyway – they had come to blows one night – but this episode was completely beyond it as far as *Ton* was concerned.

In the billet that they slept in, *Ton* had managed to get his hands on a decommissioned stretcher for sleeping on, as it was much more comfortable than the beds supplied. He had it placed in a corner of the billet, out of harm's way, or so he thought.

It was a cold night, and Urquhart came in with an axe looking for firewood. He spotted the stretcher in the corner and began making his way towards it, but *Ton* told him that the only way he would get the stretcher would be over his dead body. Urquhart didn't like this, and raised the axe to strike a blow at my father, but he managed to grab the axe, wrestle it from Urquhart and belt him for his troubles.

THE CHURCH STEEPLE

The Lovat Scout Sharpshooters were all issued with a special identification pass, allowing them to move around freely in the Somme battle zone. They just showed their pass to any officer or sentry who challenged their identity or presence anywhere on the Western Front.

If a regiment was in the front line and faced with a specific problem, an officer from that regiment could apply, for example, to Captain MacGillivray and have LSS snipers sent to that sector of the line to have the problem dealt with. One day, *Ton* and Willie Boa had to rendezvous with the officer who had applied for the snipers. He led them to a church with a high tower and steeple and suggested that they should climb to the highest point they could reach and observe the section of the German line that his battalion were detailed to attack next morning. This would have meant observing for many hours, in an attempt to figure out the depth of the barbed wire, possible machine gun positions and troop movements behind the German front line.

This church was well behind the British lines. *Ton* said: 'if the boot had been on the other foot, we would have passed the map references and co-ordinates to our corps heavies (artillery battery), and they would have poured a salvo or two into this tower and steeple, as the long-distance view would have been ideal for observation.'

Corporal Willie Boa pointed out the danger of this assignment to the officer in question. Contact was made with Captain MacGillivray who supported his snipers 100%. The officer was going to lodge a complaint with his own commanding officer and take the matter further. The charge was 'refusing to obey an order from an officer.'

The evening of that very same day, the church tower and steeple was reduced to rubble. The German artillery did exactly as *Ton* had predicted. 'If the boot was on the other foot.' How near or lucky can you get?

THE CEILIDH NIGHTS

Captain John MacGillivray had a very good relationship with the twenty men under him. Things in the LSS were worked something along the lines of the present day SAS, in as much as ranks didn't really matter and were hardly used – all could be trusted to do their duty without the normal discipline and hierarchy of standard British regiments.

Being from Nigg in Easter Ross, near the famous Glenmorangie Distillery, Captain John received a wooden case every month, containing 12 bottles of Whisky. It would arrive at the billet he shared with his No 8 Group of 20 LSS snipers. He insisted that every sniper be addressed by their first name, including himself.

This much-appreciated gift from the distillery was donated to the snipers to be used for cleaning the lenses of their Ross telescopes, field glasses and telescopic rifle sights, but, as Ton wrote in a letter home: 'the whisky never saw a telescopic sight yet!'

The ceilidh nights were something else, and were always organised on a night when most of the boys could be present. There was, however, a sinister side to this ceilidh in the middle of a war, as one whole bottle of whisky was always presented to the top sniper for that month.

Big Moir, a Stalker from Wester Ross, even sent home for a fiddle bridge, strings and a bow. Moir's fiddle was unique to say the least. It was made up of a petrol can, scrap wood and the bits he got from home. Jigs, reels and Gaelic songs were the order of the day, fuelled, of course, by the case of whisky. I don't suppose there was ever much left of it.

There were pipers among them too, and I'm sure everyone would have been able to favour the company with a Gaelic song or a recitation. It would have been a wonderful release from the horrors of war, and something for everyone to look forward to every month, which must have been terribly important.

THE WEEK BEFORE 21st MARCH 1918

Before the German Spring Offensive, it was a well-known fact that the attack would begin on 21st March. German aircraft dropped pamphlets showing a big German beating a little British soldier with a hammer. My father had some of these pamphlets at home. Little did No.8 LSS realize that they would be in the eye of the storm.

On the 19th and 20th, *Ton* and Willie Boa were monitoring German troop movements behind the German lines at St Quentin. From their observation point, they located a gap in a communication trench leading to the German forward positions. *Ton* remembered that he was counting the incoming reinforcements and assault troops four abreast. *Ton* was on the telescope and Willie Boa was working out how many fours would pass in a five-minute period. This went on all day. These statistics were telephoned to Captain MacGillivray and then relayed to Command Headquarters. With other snipers in the group feeding in further data and information, headquarters could work out how many divisions they were facing when the attack went in by the German assault troops.

On the evening of the 20th, each pair of snipers was briefed as to what their specific task was. *Ton* and Willie had to report in detail the situation on the section designated to them.

21ˢᵗ MARCH – ALL HELL BREAKS LOOSE.

Every sniper in No.8 Group was on stand-to in the St Quentin sector. The most concentrated intense barrage of the war began at 4.30am and continued for 3 hours. *Ton*, along with other LSS snipers, went to ground in the dugout, which was Captain John MacGillivray's forward command post. The dugout was twenty feet below the ground. Lights, stoves and candles all went out due to the ground trembling and vibrating with the barrage above them. *Ton* often spoke about this saying: 'what the hell was it like for the boys in forward positions up top when we were being shaken to bits twenty feet below?'

When the barrage lifted, *Ton* and Willie Boa were confronted with pieces of a soldier splattered all over the entrance of the dugout. 'It was like mincemeat,' *Ton* would say. 'He must have got a shell all to himself.'

All telephones and communication wires were cut – blown to smithereens. It was impossible to get messages back to Command Headquarters. Still, Ton and Willie Boa had a job of work to do. Their task was to observe and report back to Captain MacGillivray on the situation in the British forward positions a few hundred yards in front of them. *Ton's* account of the situation was: 'we could see that the slate coloured first wave of German assault troops, masses of them, had breached our front-line positions, and were pushing forwards to where we were observing. Following close behind we could see further waves of German assault troops entering our forward and reserve trenches.'

By this time, it was classed as a general retreat.

CAPTAIN JOHN MACGILLIVRAY'S TELESCOPE

The sector where Captain MacGillivray's forward dugout position was situated was code-named 'Saltcoats,' and *Ton* found himself there after the order 'every man for himself' had been given, but he could find no trace of his comrades in No.8 Group LSS. What he did find, in the dugout, was Captain MacGillivray's Ross telescope, which *Ton* pocketed so as to give it back to its owner if he ever saw him again. The British Army was in full retreat, or, in other words, on the run, and *Ton* recalled being 3 days without food.

He eventually met up with boys from an English regiment. They were very inquisitive to know what the LSS insignia was, as they had never heard of it. *Ton* enlightened them and asked if they had seen any other soldiers in the vicinity wearing the same, and carrying fancy rifles with telescopic sights. One of them piped up and said: 'yeah, Jock, there's a lot of them down that road in a chalk quarry.'

Thankfully, he found them, and with the appearance of John MacDonald, Willie Boa and Corporal Clark, from Maryburgh (*), No.8 Group were back to full strength, including their officer Captain John MacGillivray. *Ton's* account of what followed is interesting to say the least. Putting his hand in his haversack, *Ton* said: 'lovely to see you, Sir. I've got a present for you,' and handed the Captain his telescope back. He was overcome with emotion. *Ton* recalled him saying: 'we thought the buggers captured you at Saltcoats.'

The telescope has pride of place to this day in the MacGillivray family home at Calrossie Farm. The story of the telescope has only recently come to their attention. Were it not for Private 126315 L.S.S. MacDonald J, the telescope would be a souvenir hanging on the wall of some stately home belonging to a German officer.

*Corporal Clark's sister was *Ton's* girlfriend at the time, and he would cycle to see her every night while they were stationed in Beauly.

A NEAR ONE AT THE CANAL

My father always taught me that when stalking a piece of ground for deer you should train your telescope or binoculars on the ground closest to you and then work your way out from there. There was a good reason for him teaching me this – borne out of tough experience.

During the retreat from their sector in the Bapaume, Cambrai and St Quentin battle zone, the unit regrouped and were landed with the task of feeding back information as to the exact map reference of the most forward German assault troops then advancing. This was dangerous work, being very close to the advancing German forward units, and there was the real possibility of being captured by small special German patrols doing the same job as themselves.

One afternoon, *Ton* and Corporal Boa were on a high embankment on one side of a canal. Their task was estimating the enemy strength gathering on the other side, while their engineers were three quarters of the way across the canal constructing a pontoon bridge. This was obviously going to be a prime target for the artillery once they got the map reference and co-ordinates from Captain MacGillivray. Willie Boa crawled a few yards further forward, and, to his horror, looked below him to discover elements of German units spilling onto the British side of the canal and preparing to climb the embankment. Willie Boa grabbed *Ton* and shouted: 'get out! Run for it.' How near can you get to being shot or captured? Such was their hurry, that my father left his shirt behind, and they talked about the incident long after the war.

They broke a golden rule they were taught on the sniper's course back home in Beauly. Whether it be naked eye, field glass or telescope, you start at the nearest point and work outwards. They got it wrong by spying the far side of the canal first. The same principal is used by professional stalkers when spying a hill, and they were both professional stalkers.

THE FRENCH WINE CELLAR – FUN AND GAMES

During the retreat with the German Army hard on their heels, some of the boys in No.8 Group came across an abandoned building, with the roof blown off. Someone noticed that there was a cellar below the building, but the door was locked and barricaded. They reckoned it was a wine cellar, and, after breaking down the door with their rifle butts, they couldn't believe their luck.

This Aladdin's Cave contained hundreds of bottles of fine wines, cognac and champagne. The boys got stuck into this connoisseur's paradise, and also proceeded to fill their water bottles with the nectar of the vine. Needless to say, everyone was in good spirits, and the reality of war seemed many miles away.

Having had their fill, the boys got back on the road, which was jam-packed with retreating troops and refugees carrying what little belongings they had, when, all of a sudden, two German aircraft appeared out of the sky. Everybody dived into the ditches on either side of the road, including the refugees.

'You could see puffs of machine gun bullets all along the dry sand road as the aircraft continued to strafe us.'

The highlight of this incident had the boys rolling about in fits of laughter as they crouched in the ditches.

'I remember seeing Finlay MacRae, a gamekeeper from Kintail, face down in the middle of the sand road, firing away at the aircraft and not even looking up. He would load, point the rifle skyward above his head and fire. The machine gun bullets were stotting on the sand road all around him, but, thank God, he didn't get a scratch.'

Captain MacGillivray didn't hear about this dramatic event until days after. No action was ever taken. The captain was just delighted that his boys were all safe and well.

Incidentally, Finlay MacRae emigrated to Detroit after the war. He used to write to *Ton* inviting him to join him, but, eventually, they lost contact, and Finlay MacRae never went back to gamekeeping in Kintail.

THE GERMAN ADVANCE HALTS

Finally, the German advance came to a halt. The main factor in this was that supplies could not reach the forward German assault troops in time for them to break out for the final push.

The Lovat Scouts Sharpshooters contributed so much to breaking down the German advance. They identified concentrated build-up areas of supplies, and troop movements behind the German lines before they could be deployed. Supplying the heavy gun batteries with the usual map references and coordinates by long-range observation enabled the corps heavies to plaster these areas with pinpoint accuracy. This, and the rear-guard actions performed by all British regiments, brought the German advance to an end.

Ton often mentioned how he saw many army chaplains of all dominations urging the British troops to make a stand and remember their vows when joining up to serve and defend King and country: 'Stop! Stop! Stand and face the enemy. Remember the vows you made when you signed up. For king and country!'

I have in my possession the plaque that was sent to *Rancan's* family after he was killed in Gallipoli. It says on it that he died for king and country too. What a load of nonsense. These men of God should have known better than to encourage boys to go to their deaths in the way they did. What did *Rancan* know of the Turks? It wasn't his quarrel. Why did they have to fall in their millions to fight a war for those that caused it all in the first place.

During the months that followed the British Army retreat, and the subsequent advance forward which turned the tide in our favour, *Ton* found himself back in his usual sector, which he knew well. The

Germans were driven back to where it all started for *Ton* at Bapaume, Cambrai and St Quentin.

The Sharpshooters were given very dangerous missions. Apart from the usual observations of activity well behind the German lines, close quarter reconnaissance was the order of the day. We all think of the front line as a straight line on the map, but it is anything but. The German forward positions would zigzag and meander in all sorts of shapes and directions.

Being experts in the field of map reading, the LSS snipers would plot the exact positions of the German front line units, and then the detailed panorama sketch would be given to Captain MacGillivray. As you know, this information was fed back to the artillery, but it was also used by high command to determine how the war was going and initiate strategic planning – such as it was.

There were many dangers to contend with while operating in no man's land – bumping into enemy patrols, snipers, unexploded munitions – but being cut off was by far their main concern. They knew that it could happen in an instant, if your focus wasn't complete, and capture just wasn't an option for these boys.

THE GREEN FIELD AND TON'S FINAL ACTION

Days before 11th November 1918, No.8 Group Lovat Scouts Sharpshooters were engaged in long-range observation behind German lines, in an effort to locate potential targets. It was reported that a German battery was pounding a section of the line where British forward troops were preparing an attack. Indeed, the attack had stalled due to this problem.

Directly in front of *Ton*, Willie Boa and another pair of snipers, was the problem sector. On an elevated contour behind this sector, *Ton* could see a green field surrounded by thousands of troops and supply wagons of every description. He thought this empty green field amid such concentrated troop movement seemed very odd.

Ordinary soldiers may have dismissed this, but during their training in Beauly they had been taught to report their 'rights and wrongs' – things that looked right and things that looked out of place.

They were at Kirkhill one day spying towards Ben Wyvis, and had to pick one man out as the enemy at a range of three or four miles. Very few managed it, but *Ton* and Willie Boa got it. There was a cottage somewhere with washing hanging up outside it, and the man they were looking for was sitting on a chair in the middle of the washing. Something told them that this was unusual and they reported it, and this sixth sense was now serving them well at the Somme.

When the situation did not change, Captain John MacGillivray asked his boys to give him the usual map reference and co-ordinates. He in turn passed this information to the artillery, and *Ton* and Willie were given orders to observe and report the accuracy of the artillery heavy guns as the first salvos landed on the green field at precisely 16:00.

'At four o'clock, I was on the telescope with Willie in contact with Captain MacGillivray. It was frightening when the first salvo passed immediately above and over our position, but I told Willie that it was bang on target. Salvo after salvo was poured into the target area. I couldn't see a thing with smoke, but when the smoke cleared, the area was a hive of activity. I could see stretcher bearers all over the place, with medics crosses on their uniforms, bent over, obviously attending to wounded.'

When the British attack went in and captured this innocent looking green field, it was discovered that it was actually a long green camouflaged cargo net with heavy gun batteries hidden behind and below.

'The German guns were completely out of action with a few of them damaged beyond repair. God knows how many gun crews were killed or wounded.'

That was *Ton's* last encounter with the Germans. He never did call them the enemy.

THE MILITARY MEDAL

The four snipers involved in this last action were recommended for the Military Medal. Three of them received their medals when they came back to Beauly after hostilities ceased on 11th November 1919, but *Ton* remained in Belgium for a further 6 months as part of the force of occupation. He volunteered for this as he knew there would be no work at home.

The Lovat Scouts Sharpshooters were disbanded almost immediately, and by the time *Ton* arrived back in Scotland and was discharged, the unit had virtually disappeared – all two hundred of them and their officers. They existed no more, and *Ton* never received the Military Medal.

Ton never pursued the issue, although Willy Boa often told him to do so. Medals were not his thing. It was more important to *Ton* that he got away without being killed or wounded. He always said: 'I got out of it without a scratch.'

In the 1960's, Lord Lovat – the son of the regiment's former commanding officer – tried to get *Ton* his medal, but a tragic discovery was made. During World War Two, the building housing archives relating to the Lovat Scouts Sharpshooters was totally destroyed during a German bombing raid on London. Lord Lovat sent *Ton* a personal plaque for his services to the Lovat Scout Sharpshooters instead.

THE MOIDART SNIPER – 1893 to 1988

Ton lived to the age of 95, and to his dying day he always spoke highly of his sniping opponents.

'They were just as good marksmen as ourselves. It wasn't their fault that they were the enemy. It was the stupid politicians who put us all there in the first place.'

I never found out how my father felt about the men he had killed as a sniper, but I know he felt terrible remorse about his actions on the Western Front, where his observations caused heavy artillery to rain down on huge numbers of troops. A Reporter once asked him: 'as a sniper, how many kills?' but *Ton* would never give an answer other than to say: 'in Gallipoli, it was sniper versus sniper and you had a fair idea, but on the Western Front you never knew. You see, when you directed artillery fire onto a target, and this happened regularly, well, what do you think?'

Even one salvo of four shells bursting in a concentrated area of men is a frightening thought. That got to him, and he thought about it a lot.

As for the Military Medal, he never gave it a second thought, and after reading this memoir I'm sure you will understand why.

I know that the war affected him. I can remember the dreams he would have – his screaming would wake the house in the middle of the night, and drink used to put him mad – at a dance one night he stretched three guys in one go, after getting full of drink – but after getting the job as a postman he vowed that he would never drink to excess again. When he got old, he would have a single dram each night before going to bed, but that was it – purely for medicinal purposes. It probably accounts for his longevity.

He lost a lot of his hair during the fighting in Gallipoli too. When you were in the line, there was no opportunity for washing of any sort. Your hair was caked in muck all the time, and the tin helmet that they found themselves wearing only made matters worse. It was very red soil in Gallipoli, whereas in France it was all chalk.

He kept in touch with Captain MacGillivray after the war. The MacGillivrays, Calrossie, were big into shorthorn cattle, and he would write to Captain MacGillivray to congratulate him every time he read in the paper that they had won yet another prize.

Dad began work as a gamekeeper again, but the war was to continue to shape his future, as four men who had been working as postmen in the Moidart and Acharacle area had lost their lives during the conflict, so there were jobs going there, and the Royal Mail was an attractive prospect with a pension.

He was lucky enough to get one of the jobs, but then a petition went round locally against this decision, claiming that there were folk in the area more suited to the post that deserved the job more. I guess times were hard and jobs were scarce, so people were prepared to try anything to keep themselves in full-time employment.

My father met the man behind the petition one day, and demanded to see it. The man denied having it at first, so Dad grabbed a hold of him and took the petition from his pocket. One of the complaints on the document was that he was: 'only a gillie.' Dad asked the man for his pen and stroked out the letter 'g,' replacing it with a 'k,' which showed that he hadn't forgotten his Glasgow roots or his sense of humour. The next thing the other man knew, his heels were in the air, and the petition was in the ditch at the side of the road!

The local JP at the time, Mr MacPherson, wrote to parliament on my father's behalf, and received a reply that stated that John MacDonald was the worthiest candidate and should get the job, and I'm sure his military record would have counted in his favour.

He was on the Ardtoe – Kintra – Newton run for five years after that, and the gold watch the community presented to him when he transferred to Eilean Shona and the other side of the River Shiel is in my possession to this day, which just goes to show you.

He was working as a postman when the Second World War broke out, and this whole area was cordoned off by the War Office for special forces training and preparation for D-Day. Dad often had to deliver letters to Arivegaig at this time, and that meant crossing a ford bridge, but sometimes the tide would be too high, so he would have to follow the road right beside the seashore down to Gorten, and there would then be another two or three miles after that down to Gorten Fern.

There had been loads of mock battles going on in preparation for the Allied landings, and Dad was half way down this road delivering letters one day when an army officer stopped him and told him that nobody was allowed any further as the area was being shelled with live ammunition. 'There's a battle going on,' said the officer. 'A battle?' replied Dad knowingly. 'This isn't a battle,' and he began walking onward down the road with the officer in hot pursuit. Being the old soldier that he was, my father knew fine well that there would be an interval between each shell, and he was able to time it so that he could reach cover before the next shell landed. Other officers observing the mock battle were appalled to see this mad man walking across the battlefield. Little did they know.

Not long before he died, when he was in his 90s, some of the local young bloods were trying out a .22 rifle with open sights. They had fixed a match in the top of a fence post at a range of roughly 40 meters, and dad watched on, amused by their efforts to hit it. There were some very good shooters among them – some of them internationals – but, try as they might, they couldn't get near the match.

Someone then had the bright idea of asking dad to have a go. At first he demurred, but they continued to press him and he eventually relented and asked one of the boys to load the rifle for him.

Now, here is one thing I haven't told you. Dad was almost blind in his right eye because of an accident, ironically enough, with matches when he was a child, so he always fired a gun left-handed, which further demonstrates just how good a marksman he was.

He shouldered the gun slowly, while sitting in his chair, and fired. Not only did he hit the match, but he lit it too. Everyone was amazed by this performance, and they tried to make him do it again, but he was canny enough to remember his old Lovat Scouts Sharp Shooter's mantra: 'One shot, one kill,' he said and put the rifle down.

I am proud to say that his skills have been passed on to my son, John F. MacDonald, who has represented Scotland as a clay pigeon shooter at the Commonwealth Games, and Great Britain at world and European championship events. I myself also represented Scotland in my younger days, and, in our way, we have helped to keep alive the memory of John 'Ton' MacDonald, a simple crofter and a war hero.

What follows is the transcript of two interviews that John 'Ton' MacDonald gave to the esteemed local historian John Dye. My grateful thanks go to John for allowing me to reproduce this in full, and for all his help with this memoir.

3rd AUGUST 1914 – THE LAST NIGHT OF PEACE

The weather had been good and I was late returning home from Acharacle. I met two men at Shiel Bridge and we stood for a time watching for salmon running up. There was a football game going on below the bridge and a group of spectators watching from the high bank across the road.

The talk turned to the sunset, the whole sky was turning red, we had never seen anything like it before. Ronald MacDonald, Shiel Cottage, recently retired, said he could remember the old folks in his day telling of such a sky. They said it was an indication of great bloodshed.

Then Allan MacDonald, the purser on the 'Clan,' told us he'd heard at Glenfinnan that two trains of naval reserves had passed through that day and more were expected later for the army reserves.

This had a special meaning for me since I was in the army reserves. I'd lied about my age and joined when I was sixteen. One of my jobs had been twice a year to clean all eighty rifles kept at Shielbridge Hall. Once, when the job was finished early, I saw a big green box. Normally it was locked but now it was open. It was full of envelopes with the men's names on them. I quickly found the one labelled 1945 Private John MacDonald and took out the letter. It was an instruction to proceed to Kinlochmoidart, collect Private Ronald MacDonald, Langall, and return to Shielbridge Hall.

We stayed a while at the bridge watching the sunset but I didn't stay for the end of the match. I got home about half past eight. It was a fine bright evening and I didn't go up to my attic bedroom until a quarter to twelve. I was just preparing for bed, with one foot out of the trouser, when I heard someone downstairs talking to Aunty Ann. I put it back in the trouser and went down. It was my cousin Donald from Moss, Ronald's son, and he had instructions to fetch me.

He had a familiar envelope.

"What's this?" I said.

"Mobilisation orders," he said, "open it."

"I don't need to," I said. "I knew years ago what's in it."

I never opened it, it was still in the drawer at the end of the war.

So I set out walking to Kinlochmoidart. When I got there I couldn't waken Ronald at all. At that time there was a small cottage in the Square where the gardeners stayed and I went and wakened Charlie MacDonald and Sandy MacDonald, Mr Stewart's chauffeur. I took them back to Ronald's but I stayed downstairs, it was then about two o'clock. I heard voices upstairs, they were saying, "no, no he's not drunk, you'd better get up." At last we set off for Acharacle, getting a cup of tea at Mingarry on the way.

We had to pack up all the equipment at the hall ready for moving out and then we were sent home with instructions to be back at six o'clock in full kit prepared "for anywhere in the world."

I knew an old man at Drumfern, I used to get messages for him, so I called on him to leave him goodbye. I rapped a few times at the door and at last he opened it.

"What are you doing here?" he shouted. "Who's that? What do you want?"

"Good heavens, do you not know Ton?"

"Good God," he said, looking at the uniform and bayonet, "what's wrong?"

"I don't know, John, we've to report to Acharacle and then

headquarters at Beauly."

"If you wait a couple of minutes I'll come down with you."

As we arrived at the hall, two horse-drawn carriages drew up carrying men from Strontian and Ardgour, with a couple from Onich and one from Kinlochleven to make up the fifty.

There were quite a few that came to see them off and they'd had some 'jollification' at Salen Hotel. Everyone had a bottle, which was passed round. You had to put your tongue in it or you couldn't go to the war at all! It was a great gathering, everyone was very excited. It wasn't like that in 1939 because everyone had memories of the war, but in 1914 the South African war seemed to be a long way away.

By now it was light, the night was over.